In Memoriam

Discovery Press

First Published 2012 by

Discovery Press
5th Floor,
Tower Building
University of Dundee,
DD1 4HN

www.dundee.ac.uk
www.literarydundee.co.uk

ISBN: 978-1-84586-139-1

Design by Chris Collins
www.redlavadesign.co.uk

This book is dedicated to the Silent Teachers

CONTENTS

ILLUSTRATIONS

INTRODUCTION

BY KIRSTY GUNN

The University of Dundee has a lovely tradition, at the beginning of the New Year, of welcoming all its new Professorial staff by inviting them to introduce themselves to their colleagues and students across all disciplines and to the community at large in what are known as the Discovery Day Inaugural Lectures.

As a new Professor myself in 1997 I had the good fortune to have my Inaugural 'gig' in the same schedule as Ian Parkin, Professor of Clinically Applied Anatomy within the Cuschieri Skills Centre at Ninewells, who spoke, in his lecture, of the importance of the human body as a site for understanding and furthering our enquiry into anatomical science. Only the actual body would do, said Professor Parkin. No simulacrum or virtual computer generated version could grant the student and scientist such access to the mystery of our limbs and bones and organs. No plasticised look-alike could stand in for the vulnerabilities of our tissue and skin and flesh.

Professor Parkin spoke movingly and with conviction – I remember well – about the solemnity of the human body after death. The way it could give itself up to the scientist's gaze. The way it might allow us to probe and query. He was sensitive, to the core, about the ethical issues surrounding human life into death and spoke of the shadowy facts of anatomical research that in the past have been cast over with gothic stories of grave robbings and cadaver theft. Yet what came from that dark history was enlightenment, he said: That we could all go to the human form now without the prejudice or embarrassment that used to hold such power over our imagination. That by knowing more about the body we could know more about ourselves.

I found everything that Professor Parkin spoke about to be empowering and engaging and, as a writer and artist, potent with ideas of creativity and form: How the body is, after all, the beginning and end of all our dreaming… So when Anna Day, Director of Literary Dundee, mentioned to me her idea of producing a book based on those who had willingly given this precious gift to research, we started to plan how my creative writing students might be brought into this scientific world, to make work in response to the inheritance each and every one of us come to, in the end: our own body's narrow coffin.

The pages of this book, in so many ways, are a continuation of the same project we started together then, that, over these past five years, has developed to bring art and science together at the University of Dundee. Here in these pages are a range of internationally known writers and poets and artists who have all taken as a point of departure a consideration of the end of life. From the beautiful cover and creative sculptural work of Calum Colvin, whose sequence of photographs give us a haunting image of moving from light to shadow, to the opening essay by John Carey that reminds us in vivid, leaping words how the poetry of John Donne started in his understanding of and feeling for the body's mysteries and power… Life and death make sense of each other here, in this book. There is a grief-shadowed tablet of poetry by Christopher Reid, a story by Alan Warner that slips in and out of genre in a way that is as subtle and strange as the subject it seeks to embrace. There is an elegy, of sorts, in the piece by our University Minister Fiona Douglas, and another kind of elegy is considered in Aidan Day's response to Tennyson's resounding epic of grief and loss, "In Memoriam". And, in the way of all our cultural activities at Dundee, along with the well known are the new talents – creative writing students, medical students – who have also been asked to share their imaginations, their questions, with you and make, out of the facts of science, art.

We invite you to enjoy all these pieces as you would the contents of any good anthology and to use "In Memoriam" as part of your own contemplation of the role the body plays in our lives. Throughout the volume, thanks to Professor Sue Black and her tireless support of this and other projects that bring anatomy and literature together, you will also be able to read Eddie Small's thoughtful and moving accounts of various people who have decided to donate their bodies to scientific research - and you'll see a section at the back of the book that gives details on how one may go about setting up this process.

For this is how we hope "In Memoriam" may continue to serve our community and our future long after its words have dissolved in our minds: That we may use this collection of essays, poetry and creative work as the start of a process that may bring all of us to consider how best we may use the facts of ourselves for the good of future generations. How best, to paraphrase the words of the Renaissance poet John Donne, we can continue to play our part in this world:

"When we are to bodies gone."

Kirsty Gunn
Professor of Writing Practice and Study
University of Dundee

CAMERA LUCIDA

BY CALUM COLVIN

The series of images here collectively entitled 'Camera Lucida' were made especially for this publication, In Memoriam. They are based on one of a series of eighteen drawings from 1508 by the Renaissance master Albrecht Dürer, entitled 'Head of an Apostle'. The drawings were made in preparation for the Heller Alterpiece in Frankfurt, which was destroyed by a fire in 1729. The series include the famous 'Praying Hands (of an Apostle)', said to contain pathological features of the artist's own hands (possibly rheumatoid arthritis).

The title 'Camera Lucida' refers to the processes of creation, revelation and disintegration inherent in art as well as life. A camera lucida is an optical device used to superimpose an image of the subject being viewed upon the surface on which the artist is drawing. This allows the artist to trace key points of the scene on the drawing surface. The name 'camera lucida' (Latin for 'light chamber") recalls the much older drawing aid, the camera obscura (Latin for 'dark chamber').

This movement between light and dark, lucida and obscura, is also the metaphorical journey the works explore. In many ways the processes entailed in my method of working replicates this sense of transformation and I often attempt to incorporate this in the physical characteristics of the work. In this series is the suggestion of presence and absence – the work/image is there at all times, although our experience of it's presence is fragmentary.

Camera Lucida is also the title of a highly influential book published in 1980 by the French philosopher Roland Barthes. It is written as an inquiry into the nature and essence of photography as well as a eulogy to Barthes' late mother and is as much a reflection on death as it is on photography. Barthes talks of the studium and the punctum - the detail that catches the eye, jogs the memory, arouses tenderness - 'that accident which pricks, bruises me.'

Searching for an image of his mother that could give him comfort, Barthes goes looking for her among old photographs; time and again the face he finds is not quite hers, as he remembers her. At last, he discovers her true likeness in a picture of her as a child aged five, taken in a winter garden in 1898.

The punctum in the works presented here is represented by the series of private and personal photographs of donors, which punctuate the individual works and the publication.

My thanks go out to the relatives who generously supplied these images of their loved ones for this project.

Calum Colvin
Professor of Fine Art Photography
University of Dundee

JOHN CAREY

JOHN DONNE
AND THE BODY

What is the relationship between our body and our mind? How can a physical, material thing – the body – produce thoughts and ideas? These questions intrigue and baffle today's brain-scientists and philosophers, but we should hardly expect them to have interested a seventeenth-century poet. All the same, they did, and the poet was John Donne, who wrote what many regard as the greatest love poems in the English language.

For most people in Donne's day the answer to the mind-body conundrum was simple. Thoughts and ideas did not come from the body: they belonged to the immortal soul, which was imprisoned in the body like a bird in a cage or an angel trapped on a dunghill, and would escape from it only at death. As a Christian, Donne should have believed this, and perhaps he did some, or even most, of the time. But he also questioned it. This was dangerous, for he lived in a society that did not tolerate heretics. So he pretended to be joking, and inserted his risky ideas into witty,

provocative squibs called *Paradoxes and Problems* where they could seem harmless. What he argues in these seemingly jocular pieces is that the mind and the soul are products and properties of the body, and secondary to it, not the other way round. It is from our bodies that *"we derive our inclinations, our minds, our souls"*, he asserts in his eighth paradox, and he repeats the claim in the eleventh:

> *I say again, that the body makes the mind…and this mind may be confounded with the soul without any violence or injustice to reason or philosophy. Then the soul, it seems, is enabled by our body, not this by it…Are chastity, temperance and fortitude gifts of the mind? I appeal to physicians whether the cause of these be not in the body.*

One reason that Donne thought the body so important was that he came from a medical background. His stepfather was President of the Royal College of Physicians and when Donne was eleven he moved the family to a house next to St Bartholomew's Hospital, where the routines of medicine and surgery would have been part of daily life. According to a friend, Donne once considered becoming a doctor himself. He had read widely in medical literature, and tried to keep up with current research. It seems likely he had seen (and maybe his stepfather possessed) a copy of the greatest work on anatomy of the sixteenth century, *On the Fabric of the Human Body* by Andreas Vesalius, published in 1543. Vesalius was a professor at Padua where – since Padua came within the jurisdiction of Venice – he enjoyed the great advantage of being able to dissect human bodies, which was forbidden in most of Europe. His specimens were the bodies of criminals taken from the gallows, and executions in Padua were timed to coincide with his anatomy lectures. When Donne writes, in *The*

Funeral of *"the sinewy thread my brain lets fall/ Through every part"*, he could be describing one of the illustrations in Vesalius's book showing a human body with the skin removed and the network of nerves exposed.

Interest in the body as something to be dissected in an anatomy lecture can certainly be found in Donne. He slips into *Love's Exchange* the observation that dead bodies that have been tortured on the rack before execution are spoiled as anatomical specimens, *"Racked carcases make ill anatomies"* – not the kind of comment you would normally expect in a love poem. But he is still more original when, in line with his assertion that *"the body makes the mind"*, he starts to imagine what kind of mind, what kind of thoughts, the body would have. In *Problem VII* the question he investigates is why the most beautiful women are also the falsest, and though this seems to be just a provocative, sexist joke, the possibilities he ponders in attempting to answer it reveal something very different.

Doth the mind so follow the temperature of the body, that because those complexions are aptest to change, the mind is therefore so? Or as bells of the purest metal retain their tinkling and sound largest, so the memory of the last pleasure lasts longest in these, and disposeth them to the next.

Something within the woman, as Donne imagines it here, remains quivering and resonant, like a struck bell, after love making is over. Her body, fresh from sex, is alive with a silent music that makes her long for more. No one had imagined such a thing in English writing before, and no one did again until D.H. Lawrence. Donne's evocation of a delicately attuned body, with its own memory, independent of the mind, recalls the moment in Lawrence's *The Rainbow* when Tom Brangwen comes courting Lydia Lensky and leaves, on his departure, a bunch of daffodils.

> *…she went on laying the tray for the vicar. Needing the table, she put the daffodils aside on the dresser without noticing them. Only their coolness, touching her hand, remained echoing there a long while.*

Donne's best-known linkage of the body and thinking in a woman came about by chance. In 1610, when he was hard-up and looking for a patron to finance him, he latched on to a would-be diplomat called Sir Robert Drury. Though Drury was rather a noodle, he was rich, owning land in Suffolk and also in London in the vicinity of what came to be called Drury Lane. The Drurys had just suffered a tragic loss when Donne made their acquaintance – the death of their only surviving child, Elizabeth, two months short of her fifteenth birthday. Astutely, Donne wrote three poems glorifying her, and he was rewarded by Sir Robert with a house near his own, on the site now occupied by Bush House. Since he had never met Elizabeth, or even set eyes on her, Donne was able to give his imagination free rein, and the poems he created in her honour were fantasias of baroque flattery, ascribing to Elizabeth every conceivable perfection, including a body that seems to think. In the last of the three poems, *The Second Anniversary*, he writes:

> *we understood*
> *Her by her sight, her pure and eloquent blood*
> *Spoke in her cheeks, and so distinctly wrought,*
> *That one might almost say, her body thought.*

Commentators on these lines often say that they describe Elizabeth blushing. But we are not told she blushed, and the uncertainty makes our glimpse of her quick colour and sensitive face more subtle and intriguing. With Donne's bell-like women in Problem VII, we know what their bodies were thinking about – love-making, and the next time it might happen. Elizabeth was old enough for love-making by the standards of Donne's day, but she keeps her thoughts to herself.

Readers with a knowledge of Donne's poetry may well object at this point that even if he does sometimes imagine thinking bodies, at other times he seems quite content with the soul-body division usual in his day. This is true, and the inconsistency is typical of Donne. He seems never to have felt he had exhausted any idea until he had tried it back-to-front. However, even when he did write about the soul, he imagined it more like a body – more solid and material – than the conventional idea of it as pure spirit would have allowed. Some of his most famous lines show this:

> *Our two souls therefore which are one,*
> *Though I must go, endure not yet*
> *A breach but an expansion,*
> *Like gold to airy thinness beat.*

This, from *A Valediction: Forbidding Mourning*, imagines the souls as material, made of gold, and gold that, though it is beaten until it is just gold-leaf, and almost vanishes into thin air, never does quite vanish.

This is typical not just of Donne's poetry, where it might be passed of as merely a fanciful simile, but of his writing on religion and his preaching after he had taken holy orders and risen to be Dean of St Paul's. Repeatedly and persistently he speaks and writes of the soul as made not just of matter but of flesh, like the body. The soul, he tells us, *"hath bones, as well as the body"*, and, as if it were a body, is subject to *"cramps and colics and consumptions"*.

A theologian he was drawn to, and often cites, was Tertullian, a second-century African from Carthage, famed as one of the fathers of the Christian church. Tertullian taught that the soul was not merely dependent on the body but was itself composed of bodily matter and shaped exactly like the body. Unlike many theologians he did not believe that the soul entered the body at some point after conception. Body and soul were conceived and generated together. From its earliest existence in the womb, the body was interfused with the soul, and the soul with the body, in all its operations. So, for Tertullian, it is incorrect to suppose that the bodily senses and the intellect operate separately. To use the senses is to use the intellect and vice versa.

From what we have seen, the attraction of this to Donne will be obvious, and in his sermons he cites Tertullian to support his own view of the indivisibility of body and soul:

Says Tertullian, Never go about to separate the thoughts of the heart from the college, from the fellowship, of the body...All that the soul does, it does in and with and by the body.

The imaginative idea that gripped the young Donne of women with thinking bodies, resonant from love making, has now transmuted into the serious and passionately held belief that bodies and souls are indivisible, a belief enunciated from the pulpit and backed up by an appeal to a father of the church.

But what Donne says in the sermon just quoted cannot be true, or, rather, it is not in accord with what he was supposed to believe, and was obliged to believe, as a Christian minister. For if it is true that the soul can do nothing without the body, then how can it separate from the body at death, and survive without the body until, at the last judgment, the resurrection of the body takes place and souls and bodies are reunited? These were articles of faith that all Christians of Donne's day had to subscribe to, and perhaps those listening to his sermon would have been so used to unquestioning acceptance of the orthodox belief that they would not have noticed that their minister, elevated above them in his pulpit, had said something that did not accord with it.

But for Donne it was not just a slip of the tongue. As we have seen, it was consistent with what he had been thinking and writing ever since his days as a witty young challenger of conventional beliefs. About the separation of the soul from the body at death, he was equivocal, as he was about most things, and he could not have become a Christian minister if he had not been prepared, at the very least, to pay lip service to it. But it is clear that there was a time when he denied it and believed that, on the contrary, the soul died with the body. This was, of course, condemned as a heresy in Donne's time, and was called Mortalism. A number of advanced thinkers in the 17th century were Mortalists, among them John Milton, who insisted that the soul died with the body. Extreme Mortalists argued that the soul died with the body and would remain dead. Others, like Milton, held that the soul was resurrected with the body at the last judgment. One of Donne's most famous religious poems makes clear that this was his view.

> At the round earth's imagined corners blow
> Your trumpets, angels, and arise, arise
> From death you numberless infinities
> Of souls, and to your scattered bodies go.

Here it is unambiguous that the souls that will rejoin their bodies at the last judgment have been dead like the bodies. It is not certain when Donne renounced Mortalism, or that he ever did. The Holy Sonnet from which these lines are taken was probably written after he entered the church, and though Mortalism was not a belief he could openly endorse from the pulpit it may have stayed with him until he died.

"*I have a sin of fear, that when I have spun My last thread, I shall perish on the shore*" he wrote in *A Hymn to God the Father*. So perhaps body and soul would die together, and there would be no resurrection. Though it was a sin to think this, he says he did.

Ever since Gilbert Ryle, in his 1949 book *The Concept of Mind*, coined the derisive phrase "the ghost in the machine" to describe Rene Descartes' idea of mind-body dualism, most Western philosophers have, it seems, abandoned the idea of a soul that lives in the body and separates from it at death. No doubt most neuroscientists have abandoned it too, if they were ever disposed to accept it. The majority of people find such questions simply unanswerable, and difficult even to think about – and in that respect Donne's inconsistency on the subject reflects a common dilemma. All the same, the belief, recurrent in his writing, that the mind must somehow emanate from the body, and that therefore it is the body that ultimately matters – a belief completely at odds with the accepted thinking of his day – is for us one of the things that makes him modern.

ISOBEL REID
A LIFE STORY

It was the early 1970s, and Douglas Reid sat drinking tea in London's Moorfields Eye Hospital along with three or four other individuals. Although none of them knew each other, the atmosphere was convivial enough because they were all linked by a common bond. Each had been summoned to the hospital in the hope that this might be the time when they could have corneal graft operations. It was not lost on Douglas, however, that it would take the death of an individual, somewhere in the country, in order for him to have the vital donated cornea which would properly restore his vision on a long-term basis. Douglas was fortunate; during the course of that trying weekend a matching donor was found and Douglas was to have the successful operation which meant so much to him, but he long remembered the unknown person whose death had allowed the operation to take place.

Douglas, and his wife, Isobel, discussed the matter at home a short time afterwards and decided that they too would join the growing list of people who were minded to donate organs. At that time corneas were just about the only part of the body accepted for donation, but as the years progressed, and the list of organs which were suitable for transplants grew, Isobel and Douglas kept updating their organ-donation registrations in order to stay current. The Reids had a strong sense of conviction when it came to repaying their perceived debt to society, and eventually, when came the right time for them, they both signed up for whole body bequeathals. This registration took place at the University of St Andrews, which was relatively close to their home near Kirkcaldy, and once the formalities had been completed Isobel and Douglas shared a grin with each other, fully satisfied that they had done the right thing.

But then Isobel always seemed to possess a rare instinct for doing the right thing. This was borne out by the fact that she became engaged to, then subsequently married and had a long and happy life with, a young maintenance engineer from Kirkcaldy after having only met him on a couple of occasions. Douglas well remembers meeting this fresh-faced young nurse from Amulree when he was earning some extra money by grouse-beating up in that beautiful part of the world. After that initial meeting he plucked up the courage to ask Isobel to accompany him to his sister's wedding. She accepted, and they became engaged to be married that very weekend. Scarcity of work in the steelworks of Scotland had taken Douglas from Kirkcaldy, via Dundee, down to Corby, in Northamptonshire, but Isobel sensed that moving down there with him, once they were married, was also the right thing to do. It can't have been an easy thing to contemplate, moving from the sleepy highland village of Amulree, cosily nestling in the lee of Craig Hulich, where everyone knew everyone, and everyone was glad they did, down to the thriving industrial town in Northamptonshire where a dozen different nationalities lived and vied in a community wrought by the steel industry and the opportunities it provided. But Isobel always was pragmatic, and wouldn't let sentiment stand in the way of her intuition, so she saw the move south as something they should embrace.

Isobel was warmed by the quality of life in her adopted town. She loved her new dwelling house, and very quickly assimilated to life in England, although it might be argued that Corby was hardly typical of England at the time because of the uniquely high number of people from different cultures who took up job offers there. In Corby, she and Douglas celebrated the births of Linda, then Paula, and finally Alastair, and Isobel, as well as taking on one or two little part-time jobs, and bringing up her precious family, found time to stand as a councillor. After twenty-nine years of productive and happy living, during which time they'd easily made a raft of dear friends, the job situation in Corby, the very thing that had drawn Douglas there away back in 1964, became fragile and in 1993 Douglas's job became redundant. With both their mothers back in Scotland getting on in years, and neither of these ladies enjoying the best of health, and with no prospect of a job in the steel industry so decimated by government policy of the time, it was not difficult for the couple to decide to move back 'home'. Douglas scouted ahead for work and a place to live whilst the ever-practical Isobel finalised arrangements in England. They eventually found a place, just outside Kirkcaldy, which was to be their final move.

In their later years, Isobel and her husband took to going to the Scottish Western Isles for holidays, something which Isobel had always longed to do, because the primordial essence of the Highlands and the Islands ever ran through the veins of this lass from Amulree. Douglas would surprise Isobel with special little trips, like the one to Tiree, but the children would get together and surprise both their parents by arranging other special holiday treats for them. Isobel thrived on these loving gestures, and she also loved the attention she was given by the crews of the various Calmac ferries who, after Isobel was confined to her wheelchair, treated her as if she was the Queen of the Seas.

Douglas and Isobel Reid didn't just share a marriage, a happy home, and a family to be proud of. They shared a closeness, a profound friendship and an unshakeable confidence, all of which stemmed from the fact that they talked through all decisions and shared all experiences. They shared the work on the extension to their house. Making the conservatory, which faces south towards the Firth of Forth, was hard work but very much a labour of love. This conservatory is a living-room in the very best sense of the word, and it quickly became the hub of their existence. All visits by the children, and by their children, were mostly spent in this warm haven of a room where bright rays cast ever-changing shadows as the sun daily crosses the skies of Fife. Even now, after Isobel has died, you are surrounded by her souvenirs, and her inviting furnishings, and the sheer sense of welcome that pervades. Isobel was an accomplished knitter and sewer, easily managing the consummate precision which needlework demands, and yet she had an eye which found deep satisfaction in nature's idea of order. Looking from the east-facing side of this conservatory-cum-living-room your eye is tugged towards the garden, her garden, with its natural wonders.

Where people collect postcards to remind them of holidays and beloved places, Isobel collected cuttings and seeds. There are Jacarandas thriving in pots, which popular wisdom, and the botanical experts at Elmwood College where Douglas worked at the time, said couldn't grow. But they do grow, and they are growing because Isobel intuitively knew they would. There are Delphiniums against a frame which yearly fulfil their promise to flood the garden in colours, and there is a thriving green spruce (Douglas swears it turns blue in summer), which grew from a Corby seed, amongst many, many other successful 'imports' in this peaceful place. But two items in particular epitomise this Eden. Douglas, under careful direction from the planner, Isobel, built an extended archway, in a style and of a substance which would not be out of place in Kew, and around it they trained a family of Laburnum trees. In the winter it is an impressive sight, but there is no need to imagine what it is like in the height of summer, for daughter Paula, the arty one of the children, has painted a quite excellent triptych which hangs in the living-room and which captures all the brilliance of colour, and light, and shade, which laburnums uniquely bequeath. And through the arch, the arch which Douglas designed to act like a tunnel when viewed from the house, sits a weeping-larch which sports a small-leafed dense coverage of greenest green when in summer bloom, and possesses a haunting dignity when totally bereft of its foliage in winter. Under this tree sits a plinth with a silver plaque which amusingly reminds everyone, and always will, of the very human lady whose garden this once was.

Isobel died as she had lived – right by the side of her husband whilst he was making a cup of tea in the kitchen of their house. There was no fuss. Isobel Reid had always been a person of strong convictions, always prepared to do what was right for her family and her friends, always well able to cope with life's tribulations, but the one thing she couldn't manage to do, right up to the end, was to give up smoking. She tried, and she harder tried, but even under oxygen treatment she would always succumb to the overpowering addiction that nicotine can bring.

When she died, the University of St Andrews was unable to accept her body donation due to being overly supplied, and Douglas was asked whether he would be happy if Isobel was transferred to the University of Dundee. The answer was never in doubt. Regardless of whichever of them had died first, this so-close couple were perfectly content in the knowledge that their bodies would go to help medical research, but which university should benefit was rather immaterial. Isobel went to Dundee, and after Douglas had attended the Thanksgiving and Commemoration service in the University's Chaplaincy, he was more than satisfied that his wife had gone to the right place. A message written and read out by Sandy McLellan, one of the host of students gathered for the service that particular day, especially impressed Douglas in a day full of sincere gratitude and respect from all of the staff and students to whom Douglas talked.

Isobel and Douglas had previously discussed Isobel's impending and sadly inevitable death in the open manner they always used, and that perhaps more people should use, and Douglas mentioned that it was his intention to spread her ashes at the summit of Craig Hulich, high above lovely Amulree. He rapidly changed his mind after Isobel told him that she'd climbed that hill a 'hundred times' in her childhood and had no intentions of ever doing so again. After much deliberation he told his three children of his new decision, a decision which he could clearly see was pleasing to each of them. The family had their own service where they buried Isobel's ashes in the old churchyard in her native Amulree. The memorial stone is fashioned from a marble called 'Star Galaxy' which reminded Douglas of soft evenings when Isobel and he would lie close to this very spot gazing at the plethora of stars in the peacefully clear country sky. It is the same place where her beloved father, Alastair, lies, and as Douglas took the occasion to read out his own words of celebration for the life and love of Isobel he might well have sensed the completion of a glorious journey and the repayment of a long-remembered debt.

DAN SHAND

NOSTALGIA

First thing in the morning. The very first thing. It's a small, embarrassing thing. An incident – cold sweat and a stiff fluttering pain in my side. Something is coming for me, something from within. This was my grandfather's house. There is a memory somewhere of me lying rigid in this very room on a camp bed, a creature lurking in the shadows. In this memory I can feel my heels press against the pole at the bottom of the bed, suspended in frustrated terror. This morning is similar somehow. There's something growing here too – festering in the alcoves and skirting boards. A climbing, voiceless screech that clings to the walls like mould. I make a move as if to rise but the pain is outstanding, so all I can do is wait. Condensation forms on the small bedroom window. Autumn appears in the brassy leaves that tap at the pane.

Miles off, a severed minute – a tendon of time that stretches and snaps back... There I am, matriculating at a university several council districts away from my parents home. Happy for some time, sad for

more. Days that are dotted with golden transgressions under northern horizons. Dionysian revelry and evenings punctured with shrills of "I'm with you in Rockland". I live as a top, nightgilded. Turning quietly mad in company and feeling my eyes come to life as the moon revolves. I wake one morning to find a fingernail missing, my breath like glass. Days of darkcircled yawning and hysterical hunger. And then, the fall. That black dog of legend that paws and howls, worse than a reflection. Endless waking and rising and being and living. Passing through glossy corridors, my mind four steps behind, hearing girls on the stairwell slipping around with Joyce, looking down at my own anatomy textbooks and shuddering. I am not a surgeon. This, so far, is all I have truly learned.

In November the time comes for our first dissection. We stand in a stuffy atrium, expectant. My arm begins to itch. Some of us cough nervously, exchange worried glances. We know what is on the other side of the door. I feel a tickle in the back of my throat and feel guilty about smoking cigarettes. Our instructor's head emerges, "It's time". The air is tepid and close and we instantly recognise a presence. A plastic sheet covers it, the shape like a mountain range with corries and peaks that hint at the form beneath. It has been placed on a table, as ageless and as constant as a landscape. We shuffle in, don the appropriate apparel with slow determination. The sheet is drawn away, and "She" is there waiting. Perhaps there is an intake of breath but the room does not notice. We have lost the last shred of awareness in her aura. The buzz of a far-off zephyr – our instructor talking. We take this in for later but cannot begin to understand. Most of us see mothers and grandmothers, some of us teachers, others dry-humoured Calvinist neighbours. The past, a physical piece of punctuation, the end – this is what "She" means. I feel a weight ascend, a pressure drop. As we gaze and consider, the process of education has already begun to grind into place.

As I lie here now I think of that class, of that warm, close afternoon – closer now than ever. Sweat dots my body and the branches still tap at the window. I look down and see, as if for the first time, my life. My infancy in my toes and my adolescence in my groin. I see middle age in the curve of my torso and old age in my joints. Her body was my body, is my body. I can see that now. The two of us shivering in our beds, cold with fever at 5 am. The two of us waiting in buildings that do not feel like home, knowing the signal is coming. Both of us giving our consent, filling in forms, signing our names, blowing on ink as it dries on the paper, licking the envelope and giving away all that we had. Both lying in the dark while the class waits outside.

CHRISTOPHER REID

PROFESSOR WINTERTHORN'S
JOURNEY

This is the last part of a poem in seventy-seven sections titled Professor Winterthorn's Journey. The Professor is sixty years old and recently widowed. The poem begins with his last-minute decision to attend an academic conference, on the topic 'Nonsense and the Pursuit of Futility in Modernist, Postmodernist and Postpostmodernist Literature and Art', at a university on the far side of the world. He arrives, but spends his time instead in private meetings, or taking walks, or reading his detective novel. When at last he hears a paper delivered by an old graduate student of his, he blunderingly insults and upsets her. The passage below follows immediately.

As the lecture hall empties, Winterthorn keeps
        his back-row seat.
He'd like to use the ten-minute break to
        examine his own state of mind –
and where better than an auditorium with no
        windows, steeply raked,
all eyes led sharply down to a whiteboard
        wiped blind?

Wife-loser, enemy-maker, sympathy-craving
        recluse,
he sits there fondling his burden of self-pity:

that most anti-magnetic of human emotions,
as he has begun to discover since arrival in
        this distant city.

And now to be pitying himself for the plight
        his self-pity has landed him in!
Help! There must be some way out of this
        trap, this syndrome,
or what would he have gained from venturing
        so far from home?
When the audience returns to hear Hans
        Nagelman

on Edward Lear, Our Contemporary,
      Winterthorn sits tight.

✺

But not for long. As soon as Hans begins,
in his Viennese sing-song,

There was an Old Man on some rocks,
Who shut his wife up in a box,

there's a groan from the back row,
some scuffle and clatter,

Excuse me, please, I have to go,
acceleration and crescendo

of footsteps through an acoustic
that seems designed to magnify

any interruption,
anything untoward or awry,

and Winterthorn is last seen
shoving through the double doors,

which swing behind him – once, twice,
a third time –

with muffled force,
whereupon Nagelman completes

the absurd rhyme:
When she said, Let me out,

He exclaimed, Without doubt,
You will pass all your life –

portentous, Freudian pause –

in that box.

✺

Down half-dark, unfamiliar stairs
and through a door he never came in by,
Winterthorn staggers like a drunk man
out into what must be
the student car park.

Clean, breathable air. Blue sky.
Sun on a concrete paddock of peaceable
      vehicles.
Students ambling to and fro
in that goofy, scruffy style of theirs
that gets less readable, less reasonable,

with the passage of the years.

Right now, though, it's exactly the thing
he wants, or needs, to see.
This campus is their kindergarten
and they are (car-driving) children:
unformed, future-friendly, free.

He stands and stares,
like a voyeur.

Or like a visionary.
Across the forty-year divide,
he feels, for once, provisionally,

on their side.

⋇

Enough, that is, to be bunking off
for the second day in a row.
Now, where to go?

I know: run away to sea.

At least, to see the sea.

His feet have memorised the map:
downhill – and there you are.
And it's not far.

Nothing in this place is far.

No wind, no dog, for company,
so he'll take his wife instead
and point out points of interest.

The idea lends his step a certain zest.

⋇

And here's the harbourfront,
where I fetched up yesterday
and, for some reason, stood

in the wind and spray
letting myself get drenched.
It was different weather then.
I must have thought
it would do me some good.

Love the light on the water now:
elastic, throbbing.
And look at those yachts out there,
catching what breeze they can.
And isn't that a four-man
skiff, or scull, or something,
heroically bobbing
through a sea that must be shoulder-height?

On a day, in a place, like this,
all activity,
even the yowling and prowling
of hungry gulls,
has the air of a dance:
an expression of delight in being.
You must know what I mean –
you, who did your dying

with such energy and bliss.

⋇

When she doesn't reply –
of course, she can't, she's dead –
he's left to weigh for himself

the right/wrong
of what he's just said.

Activity as dance?
It seems to him, in this light,
it would be hard to call
her last, immobilised days
any kind of dance.

Yet he'd felt her floating away
like the belle of the ball,
rapt in the embrace
of a rival partner,
while he had had to look on:

envious, impotent, shrivelling,

back to the wall.

❋

Self-pity again:
that foolish trap
into which he seems to fall
with all the inevitability
and gravity – pun! –
of a slapstick comedian.

So that's him, is it?
The Buster Keaton of grief!
For a moment, he sees himself
stiffly toppling

off the end of the jetty
like an ornament off a shelf.

Splosh!

But no, come on,
it's too brilliant a day for that,
with the dazzle on the water
muscularly flexing
and the fighty flight
of gulls up above.

And that boat being rowed,
through a heavy wash,
closer to land.
Which he now can tell is manned
by women: four –
plus miniature cox

perched alertly at the stern.

❋

What a surprise!
What a gift from the sea!
It's Aphrodite
multiplied by four.

(Or four and a half.)

Straining shoulder,
thigh and calf,

they pull in unison
towards the shore.

Such discipline:
to disguise the sweating,
hurting efforts
of a human team

in the lightness, fineness
and complexity
of a grasshopper -
wrong number of legs?

So? –

the flash and dash of a dream!

⋇

Which passes.

⋇

Then it's such a beautiful day,
he's not quite sure what to do with it.

The sun's in the sky, where it should be,
free of clouds and beyond deconstruction.

The sea is the sea and no more:
unironically being itself.

And the world under his feet –
no-nonsense concrete at this point –

is simply and securely
a solid a man can stand on.

Or a woman, if she were here.

That's the puzzle he can't solve.

He catches sight of a bar
with benches and tables outside.

A nice, cold – an ice-cold – beer?

⋇

Alone on a broad bench,
with a tall glass of beer
for sparkling companionship.
Auprès de ma blonde –
the voice that does the singing
inside his head,
somewhere near the roots of his neck,
sings, with truer pitch
and in better-accented French
than he could muster –
Qu'il fait bon, fait bon, fait bon!

And that's the world
spread out before him:
the sea blinging

with an impenetrable lustre
under a sun both benevolent
and indifferent,
mountains beyond that watching
faint and aloof,
and the harbour itself
with its maritime industrialia
spick and span in fresh paint.

It must be lunchtime,
because here come the joggers,
jouncers and jogglers,
in all varieties of dress,
from charity-grunge and clown-baggy
to buttock-enhancingly tight,
to make their offering
of overflowing energy
to the supreme god of light.
The light gives them life
and they return it

in an ever-hopeful cycle.

Which puts him in mind of his wife.

⸙

When a life ends –
he's fumbling for the words –
where does, not the life,
but the life of the life go?

There can't be nothing to show.

There must be more than memory
and a rack of clothes
and some documents in a box.
Mustn't there?

Lives aren't like clocks,
that one day just stop
and can't be wound up
and need to be thrown away.

Are they?

Something as complex
as the galaxy
in which it exists
must have somewhere to go next.

All that religious stuff,
the blackmailing fallacy
of Heaven and Hell,
is plainly not good enough.

But what instead?
Do these pagans,
these lunchtime sun-votaries,
have the answer:

that winded plodder there,
cheek flushed
dark as a bruise,
that springy-thighed, pony-tailed prancer?

They give themselves to the light
unstintingly;
they don't refuse
the moment's imperatives.

By vital right,
they inhabit the present,
as I believe you did
and I have seldom, if ever, done.

O absent one!

><

He's not feeling maudlin, though.
On the contrary,
a world-suffusing good cheer
seems to have him in its grip,
as he dallies over his beer.

Sip. Long pause. Sip.

Time to get his troubles,
such as they are, in perspective,
and let the beer surrender its bubbles
from what it pretends
is an inexhaustible source.

Another pause, either reflective

or deliciously blank.

Sip.

><

Auprès de ma blonde,
the voice starts up again
its simple, mechanical song.

With the sunlight on his face
and his beer at hand,
Professor A.J. Winterthorn

stares into the yonder.

><

And the yonder stares back –

Qu'il fait bon dormir.

EDDIE SMALL

GEOFFREY DROUGHT
A LIFE STORY

The wonderful Irish poet, W B Yeats, once wrote *Education is not the filling of a pail, but the lighting of a fire.* Geoffrey Drought's fire was lit at two of Ireland's most prestigious and most ancient teaching institutions, namely Royal Portora in Enniskillen, whose former pupils included Oscar Wilde and Samuel Beckett, and world-renowned Trinity College in Dublin. It was a fire which would burn fiercely within him all his life. Once his university days were ended, in the tradition of so many talented Irish academics, Geoffrey left Ireland to see what the rest of the world could offer him by way of a job and a challenge, armed with his degree in Latin and French, his Irish sense of humour and his great zest for life.

He taught in England initially, and always particularly remembered a three-week sojourn at Plumstead Secondary Modern School which opened his eyes to a world of social and educational deprivation. In addition to his areas of academic expertise, Geoffrey was expected to teach gardening, and other suchlike subjects of which he had scant knowledge, and he never forgot the utterance he heard from some pupil in the body of the class the first time he spoke to them…. *Coo, he's a 'toff'*. A short time after this, Geoffrey met Jill, a young nurse from St Thomas's in London, whilst on a trip to the Princes Theatre in London, and he and Jill started to write to each other after he moved to teach in Lyons, in France. This post was at Lycée Saint Rambert, a mixed secondary school on the outskirts of the city. Assimilation was always easy for Geoffrey, and he joined the choir in the University, and played rugby for the University too, during this hugely enjoyable episode in his busy life.

He returned to Jill, whom he would shortly marry, and to Wrekin College in Shropshire, where he taught Latin, French and Greek for the next eight years or so. Whilst he was there the college admitted a student who wanted to study Italian. Geoffrey accepted the challenge, and undertook to improve his own very limited knowledge of this language by taking 'lessons' from an Italian Ice-Cream parlour owner…..carefree days indeed. Wrekin was a good place for Geoffrey, but after eight enjoyable years he began to feel that he fancied another challenge in his career. The fire of education was burning as brightly as ever, but Geoffrey felt the need to fan the flames in a different crucible.

The obvious option (for Geoffrey) was to move into one of the education departments in local government from whence he would try to influence the delivery of teaching. He achieved access to this new challenge in Warwickshire, and gained much valuable experience there before he made the move to Scotland, to Dundee in fact, a move which would significantly influence the rest of his life. Geoffrey was awarded the O.B.E. in

1985 during a highly successful sixteen year stint in Dundee, by the end of which time he was Deputy Director of Education for Tayside. Included amongst his many achievements were the introduction of Britain's first community education scheme and the innovative use of radio to deliver distance-learning courses which enhanced the educational opportunities of thousands of people.

Geoffrey had a gift for fitting in with, and throwing his talents into, whichever community and culture he chose to inhabit, but it seems fair to say that his stay in Coupar Angus, whilst he worked in Dundee, proved to be a particularly happy, and socially satisfying, period in his life. He was made President of the local cricket club, mainly because of his 'incompetence as a player' joked Geoffrey in the memoir, and he set up under-18 and under-21 teams to strengthen the grass roots level of the game. He also took a healthy part in committees of the local Episcopal Church and generally augmented the social assets of his adopted town.

Geoffrey then moved to Wales for his final career appointment and during his eight year spell as Director of Education for Gwent he increased library services for education, boosted further education, advocated Welsh-language education in schools and managed to convince central government of the value to be gained from supporting a TV schools programme in Welsh. Geoffrey Drought shovelled a lot of coal onto the *fire* of education during his working life. He was always highly-principled, and his retirement was partly brought about by his 'disgust' at the then-government's introduction of a 'marketplace' philosophy into education. His retirement was thoroughly merited because he had achieved an awful lot to be proud of, though he would never have told you so because self-pride was not a virtue to Geoffrey.

His consternation with Conservative policies on education at the time conveniently throws up an earlier incident which does much to show Geoffrey's sharp mind and great sense of humour. He was always interested in politics, and at one time stood for election in The Wrekin under the Liberal banner. During door-to-door canvassing, which he loved, he came to a door at which he had to knock twice. Geoffrey could hear raised voices from within the house, whilst the cry of a baby was battling with the bark of a dog for prominence, and when a particularly irate looking young woman, with hair uncombed and the crying infant on her hip threw open the door, Geoffrey promptly announced he was from the Conservative Party and asked if they could count on her vote.

Geoffrey was duly elected, as a Liberal of course, and he used to make fun of the fact that he received the second highest vote of any councillor in The Wrekin, and that the only man more favoured, and therefore more popular than him in the poll, was the local Funeral Director.

After his retirement, he and Jill moved to Devon to be closer to Jill's parents. Here, again, he served the Church, this time as churchwarden, and, along with Jill, launched 'Cofton in Bloom', a move designed to promote interest and civic pride in their village. They lived in Devon for six happy years, but Geoffrey increasingly had a hankering to return to Scotland. Coupar Angus had given him a taste of Scottish country life and eventually he persuaded Jill's parents to move north with them to share a house near Crieff (Jill didn't have to be persuaded). Settling into

Crieff presented no problems and Geoffrey soon agreed to be secretary of St Columba's Scottish Episcopal Church in the town.

* * * *

Geoffrey Drought, in his later life, wrote a short memoir. It is poignant, and highly informative, and he wrote it to give his children, and their children, a wonderful picture of the people and events that influenced and enriched his colourful life. It is written with humility, and with biting humour, and with disarming honesty. Tales of his Irish grandparents, and of Sundays at their place in Dalkey after being at Sunday-school and Church, evoke very clear images of a bygone, but gentler age. Tales of him climbing trees, and dropping little twigs and leaves onto the hat-brims of unsuspecting passers-by, suggest that Geoffrey found his own way to spice up this 'gentler' age. He shared so many of these adventures with his sister Meg, and they also, and always, shared a profound love for each other.

His mother, he remembered, was 'extremely intelligent', and a great story teller, and she also possessed a wonderful sense of humour. Geoffrey, in typically humble style, considered he was 'lucky enough to inherit some of her wit', but, even more humbly, made no claim on inheriting her intellect. The characteristics of his father's which Geoffrey seemed to fall heir to included a strong sense of social conscience and a passion for fishing and other sports. His father had helped in voluntary soup kitchens, providing the poor and destitute of post-First World War Dublin with vital sustenance, and Geoffrey was always driven by the same resolve to care for those less fortunate than himself. This compassion was evidenced in his political ideals, his gregarious attitude to colleagues and pupils, and in his work for the Church. His Church of Ireland Protestant upbringing was important to him, although Geoffrey confesses in his memoir that 'I never really understood the Protestant versus Roman Catholic divide'. When he moved to England it was a fairly seamless move to attend Church of England services and Scotland gave him the Scottish Episcopal version of, fairly much, the same coin.

Geoffrey and Jill were married in the Anglican Church in Nettlebed near Henley on Thames in 1961. He had already taken Jill over to Ireland, and it was something they would do on countless occasions, but one trip in particular was to have a profound effect on the couple, the outcome of which provides the basis for Geoffrey Drought's story appearing here. Geoffrey's dear Godmother died, and it transpired that this doughty lady had bequeathed her body to medical science in Dublin. Geoffrey and Jill travelled over to attend the Memorial Service, wondering what this sort of service, without a body, might be like. Put simply, it was a revelation. The money which had been saved in not having a funeral had been put to much 'better' use by providing a celebration of her life which all family, neighbours and friends heartily endorsed and thoroughly enjoyed. Humour and respectful fun, and countless heart-warming tales, replaced the gloom and solemnity of more traditional occasions. Geoffrey was subsequently impressed and influenced to the degree that he and Jill made provision to bequeath their bodies in the same way. They approached the University of Dundee where the bequeathal secretary gladly, and very efficiently, helped them to complete the necessary paperwork.

Geoffrey died in 2007, and, in keeping with his wishes, his body was transferred to the University of Dundee's Life Sciences department.

Jill and the family were left in little doubt that Geoffrey's selfless donation had been a sensible and correct one when they later attended the yearly Memorial Service in the University's Chaplaincy and witnessed the respect, gratitude and dignity which the students bestowed on their 'silent teachers'. Jill remembers well the poignancy and warmth of some of the readings from students and staff at the ceremony.

Four or five weeks after his death, a service of memorial and celebration was held for Geoffrey in his Church. Jill arranged for two marquees to accommodate the throng of people who came along to remember, respect, and to share funny and happy tales of Geoffrey Drought. And they would have swapped individual stories about his rich sense of humour, and remembered times with him on the golf course, or in the fishing boat, or in any number of social capacities. He would have been talked about for his love of sports, both in his playing days as a rugby and cricket 'blue', and in his later 'spectating' days when his sons, daughters or grandchildren could always expect, whether they sought it or not, some very vocal 'encouragement'. Each person present that day would have had individual memories of how Geoffrey touched their lives, but all would have shared an image of the mischievous, but warmly captivating glint in his eyes.

His easy ability to engage comfortably with people of all ages, and from all walks of life, was a rare but obviously natural talent. He was renowned for his amusing manner, and then there was his lovely way with words (even the odd word that wasn't necessarily lovely). This essence of Geoffrey emerged clearly when Jill produced a beautiful passage about the husband, father and grandfather who had made her life, and the lives of their two girls and two boys, such full and rich ones.

His memorial stone, at Ochtertyre, near Crieff, will forever be a source of intrigue to anyone who happens upon it, but it serves as a constant and permanent reminder, for family and for friends who come to visit, of a man who was never afraid to make decisions, and never afraid to take responsibility for his actions. A simple entry of his name in the Book of Remembrance in the Life Science building in Dundee also acts as a permanent reminder for the very same reasons.

The man with the fire of education in his soul has a simple yet perfectly apposite inscription on his memorial stone which reads,

'His humour lit up our lives'.

STEPHANIE CAPALDI

THE CADAVER

You speak volumes, without uttering a sound.
Stripped bare and cold,
How did you get here?

Exposed, vulnerable,
We are also bared
to your secrets.

This complex detachment
that burns formaldehyde in our lungs
has us at once

standing back but placing
our hands upon you,
our respect

both clinical and systematic
but still intrusive, invasive.
You are a person

But we try to see something else.

AIDAN DAY

TENNYSON:
IN MEMORIAM

Tennyson began writing *In Memoriam*, his great elegy of love and lamentation for his deceased friend, Arthur Hallam, in late 1833. The two men had been close since 1829, when both were students at Cambridge. Hallam died on 15 September 1833, whilst on a visit to Vienna with his father. Tennyson continued composing *In Memoriam* in the years right through to its publication in 1850.

Five words in particular pulse through the first two lyric sections of the poem. *Dead, death, darkness, beats* and *beat*. These words are all present, in one of their forms, in the third verse of the first lyric:

> *Let Love clasp Grief lest both be drown'd,*
> *Let darkness keep her raven gloss:*
> *Ah, sweeter to be drunk with loss,*
> *To dance with death, to beat the ground…* (I. 9-12)

Sweeter to be ravished in memory than, as we hear in the fourth verse, to face a forsaken and faded future. Sweeter:

> *Than that the victor Hours should scorn*
> *The long result of love, and boast,*
> *'Behold the man that loved and lost,*
> *But all he was is overworn.'*   (I. 13-16)

The dominant stress in both these verses, falling on each second syllable, echoing the cadence of heartbeat, is complemented by alliterative effect: *Love, lest, Let, loss, long, love, loved, lost.* The quantity of these words tends to draw things out a little and from one perspective the measure of the lines is formal, funereal, stately, the routine of the rhythm marking the reluctant life of the desolated speaker of the lines.

But in the third verse there is harder, plosive alliteration: *drown'd, darkness, drunk, dance, death.* These signal a more urgent accent, which is fulfilled in the last clause: '...*to beat the ground*'. What might this be? A marking of time, perhaps. The speaker is *in* time, paralleling the way that his verse, in its distinctive poetic beat, patterns time. His friend is out of time. At best, to beat the ground may be heard as a ritual expression of grief. At worst it is an expression of distraught outsiderliness. Of vain desire to communicate. Of being on the wrong side of the borderline between this life and the dead. The expression carries its own sense of the futility of the action it describes. Anger at the meaninglessness of its own assault on an earth that literally consumes the human heart. This is why the *danse macabre* is invoked, because the medieval allegories spoke of mortals at least dancing with the dead. Even that seems preferable to nothing.

The second lyric section of *In Memoriam* opens in a graveyard, *'Old Yew, which graspest at the stones/That name the under-lying dead'*, and the second verse of the lyric, still alluding to the rapacious Yew, sees beating as the mortal violence of time itself, hardly to be redeemed by the poetic measure which articulates it, certainly to be imagined in terms of rooted despair:

> *The seasons bring the flower again,*
> *And bring the firstling to the flock;*
> *And in the dusk of thee, the clock*
> *Beats out the little lives of men…*
>
> *And gazing on thee, sullen tree,*
> *Sick for thy stubborn hardihood,*
> *I seem to fail from out my blood*
> *And grow incorporate into thee.*   (II. 5-8, 13-16)

Envying and sick for the fortitude of the tree, the bereaved imagines relief from mortality through becoming less than human. It is one of the most gravely human moments in the poem.

Towards the end of its one hundred and thirty one lyric sections, *In Memoriam* touches more positive tones. T.S. Eliot observed in 1936 that the poem's 'doubt is a very intense experience' but its 'faith is a poor thing'. That said, Tennyson kept faith with his love and with the act of writing his poem. He left a memorial which will live until English passes human understanding.

EDDIE SMALL

JOYCE TURNER
A LIFE STORY

I met Jackie Turner in her flat in Broughty Ferry where her mother, Joyce, had lived. Jackie showed me some artefacts and photographs, and related many fascinating memories about her mother, all of which revealed much of the character of this very interesting woman who had lived such an extraordinary life. So many things came to light, in fact, that deciding where to start is not easy, but I can think of no better place to begin my look for the essence of Joyce Turner than by considering her Christmas cards.

Not that these cards still bedecked shelves and mantelpieces in February, but Jackie, on Christmas trips back from her home in Luxemburg, never ceased to be surprised by the impressive number of cards her mother received. Jackie is an only child, and there is no large extended family that might send lots of cards, but Jackie noticed that whilst some of the cards were from neighbours and friends dotted around Broughty Ferry, many were from ex-colleagues and old friends from many, many years before.

Clearly, Joyce Turner was the sort of person who left an indelibly warm impression on very many people, and especially on those who yearly reminded her how fondly she was remembered and appreciated.

Early photographs of Joyce reveal a fetching young woman, with darkly smouldering eyes. Once, on an early holiday in the Highlands, Joyce's parents were asked if Joyce could 'see' the future by some 'Heilan' folk who'd noticed her laser-like gaze. Another time, on a shopping outing with her mother to Daly's department store in Glasgow, she was talent-spotted and asked to be a mannequin because of her looks, but her mother would have none of it.

A picture of Joyce in her very early twenties, with her uniformed brother, and her father and mother, clearly betrays where those distinctive eyes came from. Her father had the same eyes, and Joyce was enigmatic like him too. John Bulloch was strong-willed and good at sports, especially fishing, and he was a popular partner in fishing competitions amongst the anglers at Loch Leven. Joyce fished too, and was just as happy in a pair of waders as she was walking tall in her four-inch heels. Tennis was where Joyce excelled though, spending most of the daylight hours of her youth on a court. 'She only comes home to sleep' was the comment her parents would give to anyone looking for her.

As well taking after her civic-minded father, who was cited more than once for saving the lives of individuals from drowning in Union Canal, Jackie felt Joyce was also like her paternal grandfather, an independently-minded soul who had been a close friend and supporter of Keir

Hardie, and had spoken on behalf of, and raised funds for, the fledgling Labour Party.

Joyce's mother, Sophie, was an altogether quieter soul who'd moved from the rural serenity of Dunblane to the heaving metropolis of post-First World War Glasgow to marry. She was a very good cook, a gifted story-teller and an excellent knitter and sewer, but she was very camera-shy and lacked the confidence of her husband and her daughter.

One photograph shows Joyce in uniform, and this opens the door to another episode in her life. Joyce had attended Jordanhill School in Glasgow, and had once been very ill with scarlet fever. Having to watch friends play tennis from behind the windows of her quarantined room did little to quell her love for the game which she would eventually play to County standard, but that experience, plus the experience of seeing her mother eventually emerge in good health from a very long period of in-house quarantine because of TB, may well have influenced Joyce's devotion to the caring of people. Apparently Joyce knew her mother was on the mend when Len, the family collie, moved away from his vigil at the bedroom door.

A first job on leaving school, in a bank, might have seemed a safe sinecure in an age when jobs could be considered positions for life, but Joyce spurned this role to join the British Red Cross as a Voluntary Aid Detachment (VAD). The war-time period of the mid-Forties was one of great flux which brought unique opportunities for women, and saw them occupied in all manner of jobs which previously been the domain of men. It also saw women entering the Services. Joyce Bulloch, who'd given up her 'comfortable' banking job to take on the nursing of war-wounded, was first posted to Chester before being assigned to overseas operations. Initially she was deployed in the treatment of wounded and maimed servicemen, but Joyce found this particularly heart-wrenching and she was transferred to working in operating theatres where she quickly distinguished herself as a very able theatre nurse.

High on the list of many adventures, which Joyce must have seen and endured, was her being on the last troop-train to leave Palestine, and included in her possessions is a British Forces I.D. Card which shows she was in Egypt in 1947, where, by this time, she was classed as a Welfare Executive. Her next move was supposed to be to a job in a similar capacity in Greece, but the degree of dithering and 'faffing about' by those in charge annoyed the pragmatic, no-nonsense Joyce.

Joyce took matters in her own hands when the ship transporting her and many others landed at Malta en route to Greece. Joyce asked the relevant authorities whether the island had a Welfare Executive, and, when the answer was 'No', she promptly appointed herself to the role, a move which went unchallenged.

Malta proved to be an extremely interesting posting for Joyce, for it was here that she would meet the man whom she would marry, and it was here that she became a direct line report to Edwina, Countess Mountbatten. Their ensuing close working relationship resulted in an unusual development when Princess Elizabeth, later to be Queen, called on the British Forces in Malta. Normal protocol would mean that the chief officers and their wives be presented to the princess, but Countess Mountbatten, surely with the connivance of Joyce Turner, had the princess meet up with the Island's top nurses instead!

Joyce's return to civilian life saw her married, and living in Edinburgh where she had her daughter Jacqueline Ann (Jackie to everyone else, but always Jacqueline to Joyce). The marriage of Joyce Bulloch to Dr Turner lasted less than ten years and she decided to change direction and re-entered the workplace to tackle a new challenge.

This took her to Carlisle where she took on the role of Personnel Manager for a company which manufactured sweets and confectionery. Whilst her experience in Welfare and in First Aid may have helped her secure the job, it must have taken a leap of confidence for this company to have taken on an erstwhile housewife, and ingénue to the factory environment, into such a pivotal role, but it is easy to imagine that Joyce's background and references were testimony enough to her competence and would have won them over.

Joyce was a resounding success in Personnel Management, and her Carlisle stint ended when she landed a plum role with Uniroyal (then the North British Rubber Company) in Edinburgh. Their American management soon realised that it was wise to fall in with her sound and anticipatory judgement, and it was once remarked, "better to go with what she wants, or else we'll find her tied to the railings", in an oblique reference to Emily Pankhurst.

A five year spell in Edinburgh, where she lived with Jacqueline and her dog Marcus, seemed to be a most enjoyable one, but even so, when the opportunity arose, Joyce lifted her household and moved to her flat in Broughty Ferry. Here she worked for the electrical giant, Ferranti, for eighteen years until her official retirement in 1984. Her position of Personnel Manager here incorporated the additional responsibility of mediation with trade unions.

Joyce often told daughter Jackie about some of the amusing happenings at work. One in particular concerned a meeting with three men, on a day when Joyce had taken her dog to work. When Joyce loudly voiced the command to 'SIT', the dog ignored her but the men all dutifully complied.

She was invited to join 'Zonta', an American professional women's organisation, when they set up in Dundee. The ethos of this association of distinguished women is to promote the position of women in many different fields worldwide, and it is not difficult to see how Joyce would have been an obvious candidate.

Post-retirement, and for as long as it was legally permissible, Joyce taught industrial relations legislation, and shared her experiential knowledge in her field with students who were working towards HNC diplomas and certificates in Management Studies at Dundee College. She also sat on a panel arbitrating in Industrial Tribunal cases, whilst much of the rest time was occupied dog-walking for neighbours, or for acquaintances in hospital, or simply indisposed, as well as driving patients from Broughty Ferry to appointments in hospitals, care centres and outpatient clinics.

The one life-project which Joyce never managed to accomplish was her desire to write short stories in retirement. This was mainly blighted by the onset of dementia and ageing problems, compounded by the sad loss of her dog, Moss, the third collie in her life. The dog's death devastated Joyce, and she found reason thereafter to venture out only infrequently.

Joyce Turner very clearly had her own mind, and, though she habitually considered matters very carefully before deciding on things, she would always follow her conscience wherever it took her. She, as a woman, was a trailblazer, and certainly ahead of her time. The era of the sixties was, according to almost all social historians, the time when women found freedoms and took up new challenges of a sort which had been virtually unheard of before. Joyce Turner had reached that point fully a decade before. Her daughter Jackie, although it must have been a decision which brought conflicting emotions to Joyce, was encouraged to go and find her place in the world in the same way Joyce herself had done.

The decision to bequeath her body to medical science was taken by Joyce in the late 1980s. A cousin, Dorothy Bulloch, made Joyce aware of this choice, and they both opted to take it up. It made utter sense to Joyce. It reflected her caring attitude, and her innate sense of philanthropy. Her love of animals, especially dogs, and her compassionate concern for people, so evident throughout her nursing career and beyond, simply epitomised her unswerving attitude and desire to make a contribution.

Joyce Turner died aged eighty-four, having lived a full and generous life. Daughter Jackie remembers being impressed by the excellence of response from bequeathal secretary, Vivienne McGuire, and others at the University of Dundee in making a trying experience much easier. The respect and dignity shown by the massed rank of students and staff at the Memorial Service in the University Chaplaincy similarly warmed

Jackie, and her friends who attended, and it made them fully grasp the value of the contribution that Joyce's donation had made. Jackie divided her mother's ashes between Jordanhill, the area where Joyce had spent her infancy and youth, and her beloved holiday destination, the Isle of Arran, although she did retain some for the house in Broughty Ferry where the photographs of such a fascinating life capture the eye just as easily as her anecdotally-rich story captures the imagination.

ZOE VENDITOZZI

TOPOLOGY

It's organised like a stage set.
Directional lights shine down on two surgical
                                    beds -
empty, thankfully.
The props that we've come here to view
are arranged neatly on the units that circle this
mock operating theatre.

We make our way round, identifying:
a skull section;
a woman's pelvis;
a genderless foot and ankle.

We're all acting it through -
asking questions, taking notes.
And all the time I'm thinking

about how the Professor would make
an ideal replacement father,
a donor dad.
This is a thought that I'm used to
and not unhappy about.

But then he leads us to a trolley
with a big plastic box on it.
It's the kind that you put extra blankets in,
                                    under the bed.
It casts its terrible, ordinary shadow
on to the lino.

He opens the box and inside is a man's torso
stained with preservatives.
It smells both chemical and over ripe.

The professor tells us about how the process
                                    works,
about memorial services,
about laws and rules.
He peels this was-man down,
revealing his layers.

We see it all.

My father's dead self appears
and I flick between him
and the professor
and the cadaver.

I'm trying to understand something
at the edge of myself.
It's a thought I can't quite catch,
and it's gone again without showing itself.

There's a fixity
- a caught shape -
to some things,
that no matter how much they're strained or
                                    twisted,
they don't lose their real, unseeable selves.
It's like an outline scorched into an elastic now.
Like a note held, held, held -
Seeping everywhere and
inaudible.

ALAN WARNER

EACH OF US,
IN OUR WAY

A massive retaining wall supports this Edinburgh cemetery on its southern perimeter. Above the cap stones you note the pyramidal summit of a mausoleum, the crown tapped at by the swaying branches of the pavement's old trees. Beyond the wall the ground level of the graveyard is much higher than down on the street, so it is inevitable – as you stroll – that the coffins of the dead are passing your cheek, one after another through the stone. Like a Spanish graveyard where the deceased are stored up in long closets built clear from the ground – ostensibly free of ants. Often the more obscure corners of those Spanish graveyards are neglected and even foundering. In these places, mixed in with fallen masonry, I have witnessed mouldy human rib bones, their delicate curvatures reminiscent of the odd slings which dog owners use to hurl a ball across distances.

In Samuel Beckett's *First Love* the narrator tells us he has no bone to pick with graveyards, and I concur. I've spotted the girl who works in A

v

massive retaining wall supports this Edinburgh cemetery on its southern perimeter. Above the cap stones you note the pyramidal summit of a mausoleum, the crown tapped at by the swaying branches of the pavement's old trees. Beyond the wall the ground level of the graveyard is much higher than down on the street, so it is inevitable – as you stroll – that the coffins of the dead are passing your cheek, one after another through the stone. Like a Spanish graveyard where the deceased are stored up in long closets built clear from the ground – ostensibly free of ants. Often the more obscure corners of those Spanish graveyards are neglected and even foundering. In these places, mixed in with fallen masonry, I have witnessed mouldy human rib bones, their delicate curvatures reminiscent of the odd slings which dog owners use to hurl a ball across distances.

In Samuel Beckett's *First Love* the narrator tells us he has no bone to pick with graveyards, and I concur. I've spotted the girl who works in our local cemetery, picking up clients at all hours, including during the day. When she caught my eye she asked both me and my wife if we wanted to feel and so we did. There was already something dead about the inanimate, rigid satchels of silicon lodged like tumours inside her cold breasts. I told her they were great and she looked proud and pleased – and much younger for the smile. My wife asked her about the price of surgery. "A gift," she spoke – curtly. We knew not to enquire further about the kind of man who would make it. Syringes littered the grass and the pathways around her. There were no chip shops open in the area until evening and she explained that she got so hungry some days that she could taste the particles of steak or burger trapped between the teeth of her customers. She insisted it was a myth that one in her line of work never kissed – that was an upmarket nicety – besides – kisses were easy; it was the other stuff on the cold tombstone.

She was dead within two months of meeting her. I can't remember how I found that out but it made me think of those lifeless pouches of silicon within her once-small extremely neat breast. Would it have retained some warm constellation of her body heat longer than the dead flesh around it? Would this be her final essence on our side of the border?

I have encountered dead people before but each time it's in some way damaging to me – to my fragile psychology – encouraging morbidity, enlivening a tentative hedonism. I am of course afraid of them – corpses – each taken personally, somehow. A young and dear friend of mine threw himself from a high roof, another took her life at the same place, and, when I returned there in some kind of dramatic homage, the small footprints of her Doc Marten boots were still clearly preserved in the mud, I could even examine how my puppy-dog stride followed her lost steps in a deprecating, doubtless, irritating pursuit.

So I feel connected, I suppose. To the air crash victims alive at 13.44.17 but dead from catastrophic trauma at 13.44.18, to the pilots who carried them there. To my Mother and Father, also – the padding in their coffins weirdly reminiscent of garish bridesmaids dresses. I wish them all the best. There can be little doubt that by the time the last second of life clicks past we really do join ourselves with what Beckett called "That one true end, to end all others". There's a kind of relief to that thought, beauty even, a graceful state of de-illumination - like a flare alighting on a black stretch of water which seems to lift for a second, then gently withers.

EDDIE SMALL

GEOFFREY HILLYARD
A LIFE STORY

Geoffrey Hillyard bemoans the fact that he can't do this year what he used to manage last year. It's not something he dwells on, being in many ways a singularly pragmatic person, but Geoffrey does have a very candid and considered view on his own mortality which includes the realisation that the human body does inevitably age and deteriorate. The body itself, 'the shell' as Geoffrey terms it, is, for him, simply the framework that supports the human mind. For Geoffrey, it is the mind which is the utter essence of life. This divorce of mind and body is exemplified by the fact that his body disdains to achieve some of the things which his still very alert and active brain would like to get to.

Walking is one such activity. He has given away all his Ordnance Survey maps: some might regard these as cherished keepsakes of much-loved and remembered walks around the hills and glens and coastal paths, but Geoffrey believes that putting things to use for others is preferable to any sentimental affectation. He gave his camping books to a bus driver

in a like gesture, and his decision to donate his body to medical and anatomical research is borne of the same simple, yet honourable, ideal. Yet for
Geoffrey it is not grand at all, this ideal, but simply a matter of putting
something to use, and for a very worthwhile cause, which, he considers, he
will no longer have use for.

Meeting and talking to Geoffrey is inspirational. His ever-courte-
ous manner and strongly held principles seem to hark back to an earlier,
gentler age. He is imbued with a sense of fairness in all things, most especially in gender tasking, which is deeply ingrained and long-standing.
He remembers, as a child, that he and his sister were always treated and
tasked in exactly the same way. His stepmother was a remarkable woman
with an enlightened sense of fairness and equality, in both experience and
opportunity, for both sexes, and Geoffrey credits her with being a great
influence in the way he subsequently conducted his life. He remembers,
as a ten year old, commenting unflatteringly about the merits of women
drivers only to be admonished with stern words and a sterner glance by
his dear stepmother. Not for Geoffrey, then, the sense that some domestic
roles are solely the province of women, and he maintains that when his
children were young he certainly changed more nappies than his wife ever
did, and he also recalls that after tea had been taken at his Bridge group
in Leeds, quite a few years ago, Geoffrey would always be found washing
the cups with the ladies whilst some of the men wouldn't even begin to
consider helping. He could tell, by the odd comment from the ladies, that
it obviously rankled them a little, but it certainly rankled Geoffrey's sense
of fair play a good deal more.

Another person who greatly influenced Geoffrey's path through life was a schoolmaster at the City of Oxford High School. Geoffrey remembers being in 6th form there, which would be around the year of 1946, when he encountered the indomitable Jock Sutton. Sutton's no-nonsense approach, his Scottish egalitarian approach to life, and his admiration of Marxism in its purest sense, all impacted on young Geoffrey's psyche, but it was Sutton's love of play-reading and theatricality which captivated him most, and this obsession, along with a love of playing Bridge, has remained with Geoffrey throughout his life.

As well as the Bridge rubbers with his group in St Andrews, and the play-reading club which he once ran but in which he still retains an active interest, Geoffrey has helped out at his local St Andrews theatre, The Byre, and he also finds time to regularly attend Scientific and other lectures run by the University of Dundee. This seems not to be a poor list of activities for an ageing body, yet Geoffrey has also regularly attended a book appreciation group in St Andrews, and often the International Book Festival in Edinburgh, although he does think that the last occasion he was there will probably be the last occasion he will ever physically manage to go. He still is connected with the local branch of the Humanist Society of Scotland, but finds the ambiguous wordplay they indulge in and their apparent disaffection with his forthright and simple style of engagement, quite tiresome.

'People don't want to talk about death' thinks Geoffrey, 'and so they tiptoe around it.' Whilst this might seem a harsh indictment on today's society, it is nevertheless a statement of regrettable fact. Geoffrey, understands this reticence, but can find no personal truck with the notion.

The sheer inevitability of death makes him consider it to be a topic which should not only be talked about, but should also be planned and even controlled. Geoffrey's greatest aversion is the thought of losing personal dignity in some lingering decaying existence. He has a friend in Australia who is in a state of elderly dependency, and the often embarrassing incidents which he has to thole because he lacks personal control seems a total affront to Geoffrey's sensibilities. This situation feeds into Geoffrey's long held support for the legalisation of some form of assisted suicide. Indeed, Geoffrey has gone further, and has formulated an initiative that he has entitled 'SCOOP', which, in its detail, seems a very simple and principled way of approaching and enacting this controversial option. Did I mention before that Geoffrey holds uncluttered and principled views? Geoffrey fully intends to retain his highly-prized sense of dignity to the extent that he sees himself being able to arrange a date with the University's bequeathal secretary, some days in advance of his planned death, so as to maximise convenience for them. He is of the opinion that many others would take the same simple course were the opportunity afforded to them, and that is why he has developed a fully thought-out scheme which he intends taking round the country to deliver to the many interested groups which he knows to exist.

He is also realistic enough to know that some people who vocally support voluntary euthanasia when they are in good health find their interest evaporates as they grow older and feebler. His own brother-in-law is just such a case. Geoffrey fully accepts that the option of assisted suicide would not be taken up by everyone, but strongly feels the option should be available to them. For Geoffrey, having control over one's death is tantamount to having control of one's dignity. His interest in donating his body, he thinks, was probably triggered by a discussion with a lady on a train. Her son was a medical student, and she explained that he was being trained without being given access to the human body. This seemed outlandish and unacceptable to Geoffrey, as it might do to many other people, and he avowed, there and then, to donate his own body. A chance discussion with a lady from his play-reading group revealed that she worked in the Anatomy Department at University which arranged and handled bequeathals and Geoffrey duly signed up to donate his body.

Geoffrey feels that more people should do the same thing, and knows a lady in Fort William who would, indeed, do the same thing but feels she is too geographically remote for it to be arranged. Geoffrey has put her right, but he does feel the whole process should be more easily understood and the concept brought more readily into public consciousness. He accepts that overtly advertising for body donation would be both counterproductive and distasteful, but he does think that having Anatomy Department contact details placed more prominently in telephone books, where people who are minded to donate can easily find them, would be an excellent idea.

Above all things, Geoffrey hates fuss and hullabaloo. He recalls a manifestation of this when he was acting the role of a priest (in a production of Murder in the Cathedral) in Leeds. The director decided that they would not bother with a curtain call to the great dismay off all the actors save one, Geoffrey, who completed agreed it was unnecessary. Hating fuss and hullabaloo means that Geoffrey has no intentions of arranging any kind of after-death service. He accepts that the 'feisty' lady who has agreed to handle administrative arrangements for him might go to the bother of doing something but, as he won't be there, he is unconcerned. After some deliberation he accepts that there are a few people who should, in fairness, be informed of his death; seems silly to have the Bridge team waiting for a 'fourth' who won't be turning up again, or the book group delaying their readings for him, or family friends who come up from Leeds annually and have dinner with Geoffrey, be left waiting to order until someone, who won't be coming, comes, and, most of all, his sister would have to know that they will no longer be nipping down to the 'Wonky Donkey Inn' for Sunday lunch. Hating fuss and hullabaloo has meant that Geoffrey feels slightly abashed at the thought of his unique story being included in this publication.

Whether Geoffrey dies from natural causes, or by his own direction, his body will be made available to medical and anatomical science for the furtherance of knowledge and the empirical education of the same sort of student as the one whose mother Geoffrey met on the train. He carries a living will in his hip-pocket and wears 'Medical Alert' neck-discs at all times to simplify matters in case his death is untimely, so that his absolute resolve over the donation of his organs and his body can be easily re-spected. When the inevitable happens, this world will lose a character with an old-world respect for fairness, an unshakeable ethic of principle, and a wondrous love of literature, of knowledge, and of life, as long as this life is worth the living. We will be left with his body, but more, we will be left with a memory or two. He'll hate me for saying this!

GARETH CARMICHAEL

I DO NOT
KNOW YOUR NAME

I do not know your name.
I do not know where you were born or lived,
what school you went to or where you worked.

I do not know what your ambitions were,
your aspirations, your achievements.
I do not know what you held most dear,

who you loved, who you've left behind,
or what they think when they remember you:
A brother, husband, father, friend.

I do not know your name.

Still, I have seen a side of you
that is unknown to anyone else,
unknown to you, in fact, for you

have shown me what no one else can show.
And I am in debt for what you have given:
Insight, knowledge, understanding.

When I first approached you
I did so with some fear and some anxiety.
But now I survey in wonder and with awe

the intricate design of nature's most
impressive marvel. A sense of gratitude
arising from within me - though

I do not know your name.

CLAIRE MACLEARY

THE ULTIMATE
GIFT

Iris opened her eyes.
She was in bed.
Not her own bed.
Then she remembered...

She remembered when she had first felt the lump in her breast, so strange and hard amidst all that soft tissue... Then the emergency appointment with her G.P.... The hastily arranged biopsy... The hospital consultant's expression when he looked up from his notes and said, "I'm afraid I have bad news for you."

Iris could still picture Joe's stricken face when she turned to him that day.

And the journey home in the car, her mind whirling, Joe the picture of misery, his knuckles white on the steering wheel.

They had talked, then, long into the night. Talked about everything - the house, the kids, their planned holiday - everything, that is, except what lay in store for Iris.

Poor Joe. He had worked so hard those past few months to keep her comfortable: doing the shopping; washing the sheets; making little snacks to tempt her; cutting her favourite flowers from the garden to place by the bed.

Iris closed her eyes again, imagining she was back in her own bedroom at home - feeling the luxuriant down of her duvet around her, seeing the pretty, sprigged paper on the walls, the soft drape of the curtains at the bay window, the ordered flower beds in the garden beyond.

They had planned to buy a swing for the garden. Charlie, their first, and only, grand-child, was a mere ten weeks old, but there would be more, they'd hoped, she and Joe - small feet and shrill voices to brighten their quiet lives in retirement after three children and forty years of married life.

The children had reacted so differently to the news - Colin, the oldest, first questioning the diagnosis, then searching the internet for treatments and specialists and drug trials; Sam, their youngest, stricken like his father, retreating in silence into himself; Kate, the middle one, practical as always, wanting to know how she could help.

Iris gave a little sigh. Kate was the double of her mother, they all said that, hard-working and able. And now they were helpless together.

Still, Iris thought, she should count her blessings. Her illness had not been protracted and, since she had come here to the hospice, the medical staff had managed to control the pain. Of course she missed her home - her soft bed, Joe's lovely garden, her own things around her - but the hospice wasn't like a hospital, all uniforms and officialdom, but modern and cheerful with all the support anyone could possibly need.

She had felt so low at first, depressed and lonely, though Joe and the family were able to drop in at any time. But her move to Maggie's Centre had given her space to think, and the staff and the other patients there had helped crystallise her thoughts…

She'd had time to reflect - on the contented life she had lived with Joe, the comfortable home they had shared, the three healthy children they had raised.

Then, in the calm surrounds of the hospice, she had felt able to voice her innermost fears - of the pain that might still come, the death that would soon be hers - and to air her concerns for what lay after, not only for herself but for Joe, and her children, and her children's children...

She thought of the friends she and Joe had made over the years - good friends, too many of them long gone... The funerals they had attended... Dust to dust...

She knew it wouldn't be long, now.

And she had come to a decision.

She would tell Joe today.

❊

Joe came in from the garden, wiping his feet carefully on the rough sisal mat before pulling off his muddy boots. He had been digging for hours, turning over the earth in the flower beds. He found it helped, since Iris had gone into the hospice, to do manual work. Took his mind off things for a bit.

He showered and selected a freshly ironed check shirt from the wardrobe. He owed it to Iris. She had always kept him looking smart and he wasn't going to let things slip now. He looked at her things hanging there - tailored tweed skirts and silky pastel blouses and coats with soft fur collars. His heart lurched.

Oh, get on with it, he said to himself, as he reached for a pair of highly polished brown brogues.

As he approached the bedside, Joe could see that Iris's eyes were closed.

She looked so peaceful lying there, but shrunken, all of a sudden, like a flower closing in on itself.

He bent to gently kiss her forehead.

Iris opened her eyes.

"I'm sorry, pet. Did I waken you?"

"No. I was just lying here having a think. But what have you been up to?"

Joe sat back in his seat. "Well, you'll be pleased with me. I ran round with the hoover first thing, then did an ironing and I've turned over the soil in all the flower beds."

"Joe..." she tutted, " If you don't take it a bit easier you'll be ending up in here with me."

He gave her an arch look. "Would that be a bad thing, do you think?"

She ignored him. "Have you spoken to the kids?" she asked.

"Kate came past at teatime yesterday with some meals for the freezer."

"She does well, bless her, with a new baby to see to. How is Charlie?"

"Thriving, by all accounts. Tom was holding the fort. She said she'd drop in to see you this evening. Then Colin rang later on. He'll be through at the weekend."

"And Sam?"

"He's been in London, so I haven't heard. But I'm sure he'll be in touch."

"I've been thinking, Joe..."

"What about, pet? Now I don't want you worrying..."

"No, it's not what you think... Not the house... Or the kids..."

"What, then?" Joe looked at her anxiously.

"It's about me."

"Are you fretting, pet... Afraid... Of the end?"

"No," she patted his hand. "Not that... Not any more.... It's just... That..."

Joe leaned forward.

"I've decided to donate my body to medical science."

There. I've said it, Iris thought, lying back on her pillows.

Joe sat, stunned, staring in to space.

There was a long silence then, finally, he spoke.

"But why, Iris?"

"Because I've had a good life... Even with this happening to me... And they've been so caring here... And..." The words came out in a rush. "I've been thinking about the kids, all three of them... And this new baby... And the other new babies that are to come... And..." She reached out to him, "I want to give something back, Joe... Something tangible... And... And this is the best way I can think of."

Joe took her hand in his, mind flashing back to the first time he had set eyes on her - the pretty, soft hands, the dainty feet, those glorious violet eyes...

He thought of their courtship, their wedding day, their times together, good and bad, the birth of their children, their plans for retirement...

Then, as he sat there, he pictured his wife's depleted body, transported from a mortuary to be laid out in a pathology lab in front of complete strangers...

He sat there in silence for a few moments.

"Are you really sure about this, Iris?"

"Yes, Joe, my mind's made up."

✺

Steve filed into the University Chaplaincy Centre.

He wished his Mum hadn't made him wear his suit. Hardly any of the other first years was wearing a suit and he felt seriously uncool. But the 'In Memoriam' service was to start at 2 o'clock and they had been told by the Medical Sciences staff to dress soberly for the event, for they'd be there in the Chapel, him and all the medical students and staff, to mark the University's respect for those who had donated their bodies. So a suit it was.

Steve found himself at the head of the line, abreast of the front row where the University professors and other dignitaries were seated. He watched as the congregation assembled. They were older, mostly: single people; middle-aged couples supporting one another with a hand or an arm, sometimes with the aid of a walking stick.

At the end of the second row on the far side, one elderly man caught his eye - a spry, trim chap in a tailored sports jacket with a neatly ironed check shirt and well-polished brown shoes. His face was ruddy, his hair tidily combed but, Steve thought, he looked lost, somehow, as if he had ended up at the wrong party.

The students had been told that a joint cremation service for the donors had already been held, and that some of the families would have waited for up to two years for this opportunity to remember their loved ones.

That was a while to wait, Steve reckoned.

Actually, a really long time…

A hush settled as the University Chaplain rose to address the congregation - families and friends of the donors, doctors and dentists in training, researchers in Medical Sciences, staff from the College of Life Sciences and from other departments in the University.

"We come here today," she intoned, "to commemorate and give thanks for the generosity of those who have given their bodies for the teaching of Anatomy and the furtherance of Education."

The organ struck up:

"The King of love my shepherd is..."

Steve didn't know the hymn, couldn't follow the music. So he mouthed the words, trying not to catch anyone's eye.

"Doesn't matter anyway," he said to himself. "Nobody will notice."

There was a Reading next:

"To everything there is a season... A time to be born and a time to die..."

Steve couldn't imagine either.

Then a Reflection.

Then another Reading, this time from the Director of the Centre for Anatomy and Human Identification:

"How long is a man's life..."

Steve looked at the old man at the end of the far pew. How long had his been, he wondered. He must be seventy, nudging eighty even.

"And on that day he will not have ceased..." the Director's voice went on.

What does she mean, Steve thought... "not have ceased..."

Next up was the Professor of Anatomy.

His words were succinct: he spoke of life and death; of ritual and taboos; of keepsakes; of the gift of giving to others; of the pride in the giving of that gift...

He spoke, then, of that ultimate gift - the miracle of life.

Steve felt a shiver run down his back.

A girl at the back sang a solo.

Some in the congregation were weeping, now.

Others sat, grave and stoic.

Around the walls, the students shuffled restlessly.

There were prayers for the dead - and for the living - yet still the words meant little to Steve.

And now the University Chaplain was reading out the names of the donors.

The forty-one names would be recorded in the Book of Remembrance that is kept on permanent display in the Medical Sciences Institute.

"Sarah Bell... Olga Bennell... Arthur Buchan..."

Steve attempted to mentally attach a face to each name.

"Alexander Caldwell... Anne Caulfield... Muriel Cockram..."

Next he tried to imagine what sort of job these individuals could have done.

"Evelyn Hatcliffe... Owen Hearty... Angus Hood..."

Whether they were married, with children.

"Peter Jeffries... David Johnston... Mairianne Kean..."

Steve thought back to his secondary school, to the teacher who had urged him to try for University. He reflected on the sacrifices his Mum had made, bringing him up as a single parent. He remembered his embarrassment, that first day at Uni, all the other kids so confident and cool.

"Mary Large... Helen Leiper... Francis Lomas..."

He thought about the terror that would await him the following Monday in the Pathology Lab, when he would have to handle a body part for the very first time...

Then his attention swung back all those men and women who had given their bodies - the 'silent teachers' someone had called them.

"George McEwan... John McGregor... Phyllis McQuillan..."

His mind leapt forward to the day of his graduation - to all the good he, too, could do when, finally, he qualified as a doctor.

"Richard Melville... Leonard Minto..."

Something made Steve glance across at the old man who sat, perfectly still, his eyes fixed on the single coffin.

"Iris Mitchell..."

And at that moment, as if in acknowledgement, the man turned his head and looked back at Steve.

"We remember..." The Director said.

FIONA DOUGLAS

OUR SILENT
TEACHERS

Standing in an Anatomy Lab for the first time as a University Chaplain is a profound and humbling experience. Nothing can prepare you adequately to meet the world of wonder about to unfold. I gathered with an anxious group of students round the body that would give them their greatest gift of learning over the next year.

Towards the end of the academic year, the University of Dundee holds a Service of Thanksgiving for those who donated their bodies for the teaching of Anatomy and the furtherance of medical education. This is one of the most important and poignant services to be held in the University Chapel as it brings together the families of each individual donor, every first year medical and dental student, young men and women preparing for work and research in the medical sciences, staff from the University, and Her Majesty's Inspector of Anatomy for Scotland.

Commemorating the lives of some fifty people is a responsible and somewhat difficult task but it is also an immense privilege. Each family has its own experience of grief: some may not fully appreciate, understand or accept the choice made by their loved one to donate their body for the purposes of teaching; some may not have had to the chance to say goodbye properly; and others may have done so already. It is also an emotional day for the students who, for the first time, will meet the families of the donors.

Death is a harsh reality to come to terms with and we are not helped by smooth words spoken from a safe distance but by those who share the loss with us, taking time to reflect and remember the way in which those who have died have touched our lives. It is therefore within this pastoral context that a Christian service takes place acknowledging that people of all faiths and none are very welcome. Hymns and readings are chosen with great sensitivity and care. For many families this will be the funeral service for someone they loved very much and the only opportunity they may have to say goodbye properly. In recognition of this, a single coffin is present, representing all those who bequeathed their bodies. The Chapel is always full, with students quietly and solemnly round the gathering of seated relatives, friends and staff.

The service begins with the acknowledgment that we come together to express our sorrow and sadness, to rest with quiet heart, to find comfort and strength. Alongside expressions of grief is the opportunity to re-member and give thanks for those who in death have served the living. Gratitude for this priceless gift is embodied in the readings and reflec-tions from staff and students. The main part of the service is centred on reading out the names of each donor. Honour and respect are given to each individual in this act of remembrance and this is followed by the

words of committal. The service closes with the encouragement to look to the future. It is an important time for families to experience healing and closure and for students to acknowledge that wherever they go in the world, whatever they do, the debt they owe to those who have given themselves in this way can never be measured.

Conducting the service each year, I am always deeply moved both by the feeling of unity and community which come from the relatives whose shared pride is tangible, though their individual sense of loss is as manifest as in any service of commemoration, and by the profound appreciation shown by the students. For those who have lost loved ones, the personal reflections given by the students provide words of hope and comfort which resonate long after the service is over. This is best summed up in the words of tribute from one group of students:

The human body is the most precious source of knowledge in all medical science. Amidst medicine's dazzling array of technology, nothing can equal the human body in giving students of medicine their fundamental knowledge of anatomy. Our silent teachers, as that is what they were, provided us with a text that no book could duplicate, no series of lectures could match and no computer could simulate. Our medical learning stems from this understanding and the donation of one's body for the teaching of anatomy literally becomes the gift of life.

If anatomy alone were the only thing that these students learned, this would have been significant in itself. However, over the years from the tributes I have heard, I am aware that these students learn much, much more. In addition to anatomy, they learn about the human attributes which are the heart of soul of medicine. As our students have been the recipients of a charitable act of giving, they are moved by this extraordinary ability to give to others and they are touched by compassion to consider and care for the needs of another. This gives our students a great empathy towards the donors; wondering about the life they lived, what motivated them to make such a gift. Encompassing all this is the sense of wonder and awe that comes from an appreciation and understanding of the human body – the crown of creation. Charity, compassion, empathy, sensitivity, curiosity, wonder and awe are the attributes of a caring person. They are also the vital characteristics of a good physician. Our students summed this up in a tribute:

During this past year we have come to understand something of those who have donated their bodies in the way they have, of their beliefs and motives, their altruistic reasoning, and this has made us look inward towards ourselves – our own mortality and inadequacies. Leading by example, not only have they given us a unique understanding of anatomy but also allowed us to be more compassionate and selfless.

What has passed from the lives of the donors into the lives of our students has the power to awaken, to impel change and to expand the heart. It is one of the greatest gifts to be given.

Standing alongside students on the first day in the anatomy lab is indeed a profound experience. Standing with them in the Chapel at the end of the year gives me immense pride, expressing heartfelt gratitude for those being commemorated and for the goodness of grace that makes all these things possible.

To return, finally, to the words of our own students:

We will be forever humbled and indebted by the final and gracious gift of those who have donated their bodies for the work of science. These "silent teachers" have shone a bright light onto the path of discovery we have under-taken - and without their help our understanding of anatomy and what it is to be human would be incomplete.

EDDIE SMALL

THE BEQUEATHAL
SECRETARY

The importance of the donation of bodies to medical research and teaching cannot be overstated. Generation upon generation of students from the fields of Anatomy, Dentistry, Medicine and Surgery, owe a huge debt to those selfless people who bequeathed their bodies, and every person in Scotland and beyond has benefitted enormously from the advancement in techniques and technology which has emanated from the work and the discoveries of the dedicated students and staff who turn first to the human body to learn everything they need.

The Scottish Government acknowledges this worth, and pays the subject of the bequeathal of bodies the utmost respect, by uniquely appointing an Inspector to uphold the most stringent of standards across the five relevant universities in Scotland. *HM Inspector of Anatomy in Scotland*, Professor Robert Wood, properly demands that the Universities of Dundee, St Andrews, Edinburgh, Glasgow and Aberdeen meet these standards in every aspect. He controls the licensing of certain individuals to maintain exemplary standards of practice in each University, and licenses are not given without extremely careful consideration, but he also oversees the necessary administration within each site. In the University of Dundee, as in other Scottish universities, the administration is undertaken by a Bequeathal Secretary, and the person entrusted with this role in Dundee is Mrs Vivienne McGuire.

Asked about the job she does, Vivienne underplays its importance, but a five minute discussion on the role of Bequeathal Secretary reveals both her mastery of understatement and her commitment to the ethos of the Scottish Government and the University of Dundee. The secretary, she explains, arranges the sending of *Declaration of Bequest* forms to people who have requested them. This request often comes through an initial telephone call from the person who intends making this bequest, or through the GP or solicitor of the person. Vivienne is the initial contact, and many of those who go on to donate their bodies will have spoken to her at the outset, and her informed, friendly and empathetic manner has doubtless helped many through this stage.

Once the form has been completed, duly witnessed, and returned, the Bequeathal Secretary starts a new file. All files in Dundee are meticulously kept, and they are maintained in alphabetical order of surname rather than by number; Vivienne insists that each refers to a person which explains why she is happy to incur extra work in order to personalise the files. *HM Inspector of Anatomy in Scotland* regularly checks these files, as part of his own remit, and Vivienne welcomes this as it validates her own belief in the importance of excellent practices. Occasionally, someone who has completed a form, or a relative of such a person, might ring, or

even call in, to ask a question, update file information or gain some sort of reassurance, and again the Bequeathal Secretary is on hand to answer questions and maintain the personal contact on behalf of the University.

Inevitably we all die, and when someone dies who has bequeathed their body the Bequeathal Secretary organises a sequence of events. The call may come from a relative of the deceased, or from a solicitor or funeral director, but it more often comes from the GP or from the hospital that had been taking care of the individual, or the care home where death has occurred. The Anatomy Act of 1984 (as amended 2006) demands that the next-of-kin, or executors, of the deceased complete a duly witnessed Authorisation Form (this goes under the unwieldy title of *Authorisation for use of a Body for Anatomical Examination*). These are sent, or handed, to relatives or executors, and it is not unknown for Vivienne to guide people, even to the extent of visiting them in their homes, through this potentially trying stage. The University of Dundee has facilitated a 'Relatives' Room' in the Life Sciences Building, where Vivienne is at hand with a reassuring word or just a cup of tea for any relative who calls at this time. She also has to obtain the *Medical Certificate of Cause of Death*, again controlled by the Anatomy Act 1984, signed by a registered medical practitioner, and she is bound to send a Form of Notice to *HM Inspector of Anatomy in Scotland*. The Bequeathal Secretary also advises the College of Life Sciences in the University.

Vivienne also requires to have (another form) instructions from next-of-kin, or executors, for the final disposal of remains. This instruction is retained in the pristine filing system, and, at the appropriate time, this form is the basis of her starting the organisation of the funeral with the Funeral Director and the Crematorium, and for the intimation and invitation to relatives. There are options open to relatives about the funeral, and, again, Vivienne is prepared, and happy, to talk this over with relatives as necessary.

As Bequeathal Secretary at the University of Dundee, Vivienne has two other particular duties, both of which give her a sense of personal pride. For all those whose next of kin have given their consent to do so, Vivienne adds their names, in tribute to their ultimate gift, to the University Roll of Honour, which is proudly and prominently displayed in the College of Life Sciences in the University. Relatives are welcomed to come and read this Book if they desire, and students pass by the glass-encased tribute day and daily, and are often seen stopped in silent acknowledgment. Vivienne also liaises with the University Chaplaincy when it comes to organising the 'College of Life Sciences Thanksgiving Service' held in May every year. As well as supplying the Chaplain with the names of those generous people who donated their bodies, Vivienne contacts their relatives. And she attends the Service, and like everyone else who attends, and this includes Professor Robert Wood, she stands in awe and admiration at the selfless gift of those whose names are read out, and at the respectful solemnity of the students who pack the service room. She shares the potency of this occasion, but, uniquely, as Bequeathal Secretary, Mrs Vivienne McGuire feels a sense of completion in that she has been involved since the initial call, and the sending out of the first form, until the day of the Service of Thanksgiving'. And her own degree of respect is constantly displayed in the very personal, yet stringently professional manner in which she has handled and conducted each and every stage of the process.

It's just her job, she'll tell you – but what a job she and her fellow Bequeathal Secretaries do!

Contact with any of the individual secretaries can be made by calling
Richard Dimelow at St Andrews House in Edinburgh on 0131 244 5184
or by e-mail at: richard.dimelow@scotland.gsi.gov.uk

BIOGRAPHIES

EDDIE SMALL *helps deliver the Creative Writing programme to Dundee students but also does copywriting for LiteraryDundee's website, (www.literarydundee.ac.uk). He is currently undertaking a History PhD at the University of Dundee on the culture of death in Scotland and has quite recently accepted an invitation to represent academia on a government-backed steering group entitled Good Life, Good Death, Good Grief. Amongst published articles his work has been in New Writing Dundee on three occasions.*

Born in Glasgow in 1961, CALUM COLVIN *is Professor of Fine Art Photography at Dundee University. His work is held in numerous collections including the Metropolitan Museum of Modern Art, New York; The Museum of Fine Art, Houston; Tate Britain and the Scottish National Portrait Gallery, Edinburgh. A practitioner of both sculpture and photography, Calum brings these disciplines together in his unique style of 'constructed photography': assembled tableaux of objects, which are then painted and photographed.*

KIRSTY GUNN *has been the Chair of Creative Writing at the University of Dundee since 2006 and is co-director of Literary Dundee. As well as being instrumental in introducing the very successful Literary Salon series to Dundee, and helping to develop the Dundee Literary Festival, Kirsty has managed to devote time to her own writing. Her published works include* **Rain (1994),** **The Keepsake (1997),** **This Place You Return to is Home (1999),** **Featherstone (2002)** **The Boy and the Sea (2006)** *and* **44 Things: A Year of Life at Home (2006).**

ANNA DAY *is the Director of Literary Dundee, www.literarydundee.co.uk, an umbrella organisation that includes the Dundee Literary Festival (which she founded), the Dundee International Book Prize, Dundee Literary Salons, New Writing Dundee, Dundee Writes and many* other activities. She is also the Publishing Manager of Dundee University Press (www.dundee.ac.uk/dup). Married with two small daughters, in her rare spare time she writes fiction. Her starting point for this book was the idea that from every life comes a story that should be told.

CHRIS COLLINS has, for quite a long time now, been a designer of all types of printed material. Following a long London-based career in publishing, he fled the metropolis to start a new life and concentrate on book design of all kinds, including ebooks. He also designs and makes furniture and has a workshop in Fife. He can be contacted through www.redlavadesign.co.uk.

JOHN CAREY is a Fellow of the British Academy and was Merton Professor of English Literature at Oxford from 1975-2001. He is now an Emeritus Professor. He has been principal book reviewer for the Sunday Times since 1977, and has chaired the Booker Prize judges twice, in 1982 and 2004. His books include **Milton** (1969), **The Violent Effigy, A Study of Dickens' Imagination** (1973), **Thackeray, Prodigal Genius** (1977), **John Donne, Life, Mind and Art** (1981), **Original Copy** (1987), **The Intellectuals and the Masses** (1992), **Pure Pleasure** (2001) and **What Good are the Arts?** (2005).

DAN SHAND became an Honours Graduate of the University of Dundee in 2011. His success in the Creative Writing modules led to short stories being published in New Writing Dundee and Dundee Writes, and he is now undertaking an MLitt in Creative Writing at the University of Edinburgh.

CHRISTOPHER REID was educated at Exeter College, Oxford, where he won a place to read English in 1968. His early poetry was published in many august publications such as the Listener, Ian Hamilton's New Review and the New Statesman. His first published collection was **Arcadia** in 1979, followed by **Pea Soup** in 1982. He won the Costa Book of the Year prize in January 2010 for **A Scattering**, a moving collection of poems of tribute to his late wife. Later in 2010, Reid's book-length poem **The Song of Lunch**, about the meeting of two former lovers, was made into a BBC film starring Emma Thompson and Alan Rickman.

STEPHANIE CAPALDI is a third year medical student. In first year, all medical students are asked to consider their feelings toward the cadavers and to determine in that response how the study of anatomy is of benefit to their learning. While writing her piece, Stephanie, like many of her fellow students, found that her primary reaction was one of gratitude.

AIDAN DAY *was Professor of English at the University of Edinburgh and at the University of Aarhus, Denmark, before moving to Dundee, where he takes part in teaching on the Mlitt in 'Writing Practice and Study'. His books include* **Romanticism** *(1990; 2nd edition forthcoming 2011);* **Angela Carter: The Rational Glass** *(1998); and* **Tennyson's Scepticism** *(2005). He has co-edited a 31-volume facsimile edition of Tennyson's poetical manuscripts,* **The Tennyson Archive** *(1987-93). He is currently writing on the song lyrics of Bob Dylan.*

ZOE VENDITOZZI *has recently completed the MLitt in Creative Writing at Dundee University. One of the first creative criting students to visit the anatomy department, she afterwards described the experience as "inspirational and deeply moving". A finalist in the Dundee International Book Prize, Zoe's debut novel, 'Anywhere's Better Than Here' will be published by Sandstone Press later this year. She is currently working on a collection of short stories and a new novel.*

ALAN WARNER *was already the author of five previous novels:* **Morvern Callar**, **These Demented Lands**, **The Sopranos**, **The Man Who Walks** *and* **The Worms Can Carry Me To Heaven**, *when his newest book,* **The Stars in the Bright Sky**, *which was long-listed for the Booker Prize, was published in 2010. In 2003 he was chosen as one of Granta's twenty Best of Young British Novelists. Morvern Callar and The Sopranos have been made into feature films.*

GARETH CARMICHAEL *is a fourth year medical student at Dundee. This poem came as a response to a challenge set to medical students to encourage creative expression. For Gareth, it rekindles a childhood interest in creativity and he intends to keep writing and to explore the surprisingly symbiotic relationship between science and creativity as part of his ongoing studies to be a doctor.*

Glasgow born, CLAIRE MACLEARY *worked as a training consultant, antiques dealer and entrepreneur before embarking on a MLitt in Creative Writing at Dundee University, which she has recently completed. Several of her short stories have been published.Fiona Douglas is the*

Chaplain to the University of Dundee. She gained her PhD from Edinburgh University and was awarded the MBE by the Her Majesty the Queen for services to Higher Education in 2007.

FIONA DOUGLAS *conducts the Thanksgiving Service each year for those who donate their body for the teaching of Anatomy and furtherance of medical education. She has a published article, written in 2009 as a shared effort with Dr Jeremy Crang, entitled: 'Worship after War: The Gulf Service of Remembrance and Thanksgiving 1991' in an anthology called Worship and Liturgy in Context.*

VIVIENNE McGUIRE *is the University of Dundee Bequeathal Secretary.*

DONATING YOUR BODY

Donating your body to Medical Science is a selfless and generous thing for any one of us to do, and there is a constant and increasing need for donors, particularly since new surgical training has been so successfully implemented in Scotland. If you are minded to consider donating your body to help further the cause of medical science, contact Vivienne McGuire at The University of Dundee.

Alternatively, if you prefer, you can contact one of the other University Medical Schools listed here.

Sandra Dye, Department of Anatomy
University of St Andrews, St Andrews KY16 9TS
01334 463 596, sd4@st-and.ac.uk

Vivienne McGuire , Faculty of Life Sciences
University of Dundee, Dundee DD1 5EH
01382 388 825, v.mcguire@dundee.ac.uk

Margaret Moir, Department of Anatomy
University of Aberdeen, Aberdeen AB25 2ZD
01224 274 320, m.moir@abdn.ac.uk

Fiona Mowat , Department of Biomedical Sciences
University of Edinburgh, Edinburgh EH8 9XD
0131 650 2997/8318, F.Mowat@ed.ac.uk

Ann Mellish, The Anatomy Department
University of Glasgow, Glasgow G12 8QQ
0141 330 4296, a.mellish@bio.gla.ac.uk

This book was made possible by the following organisations:

 *Literary Dundee*

 *University of Dundee, External Relations*